SYMBOLICALLY SPEAKING

by

D. Douglas Schneider

Printed and published in the
United States of America

First edition

For additional copies write to:
World Peace University
35 S. E. 60th Ave.
Portland, OR 97215

ISBN # 0-939169-01-0

FOREWORD

Modern man is in danger of losing harmony with the rhythms of nature. He also tends to forget his own past. Thus, he gets out of balance and finds himself isolated. He cannot appreciate the slow growth of a flower and wants to speed it up for commercial reasons. He loses the ability to celebrate and to enjoy, to relax and be really happy.

The church year is a most valuable reminder of the cycles in which our life is to occur. But most of us forget its meaning, the deep symbolism in our festivals and celebrations, the wisdom in old customs which the younger generation is about to forget. We live, however, in these customs, and tradition again and again asks us to keep the questions of the meaning of life and death, of growth and love alive, so that we mature in faith. That is important, indeed, it is the most meaningful part of education.

The author of this valuable book leads us through our own childhood, traces many forgotten experiences and helps to make conscious what most of us still have only a vague idea about. He writes neither for children only nor for adults only, but wants to encourage families to share in the little delightful stories he is telling us on every page.

What is really required is that families come together in order to share what the Good News means in their daily lives. The integrity of the family is weakened precisely because many parents do not know how to "say it", and the generation conflict is increasing the gaps of communication about the real questions of life. Mother Teresa of Calcutta used to say: "A family which prays together stays together." That is true. And the author wants to help us precisely in this difficult venture — to reflect our daily life in the light of the history of God with his people, in the light of prayer and reflection.

God loves the children also through the love and care of parents. And God teaches the parents also through the questions and worries of their children. This exchange is what constitutes the family. And this is what is required today more than ever before.

Michael von Brück
Madras/India

PREFACE

This book was a long time in the making. Since 1971 in Marine City, Michigan, I have told stories to children during the Sunday worship service. I recognize that sometimes the adults get more than the children, and that is okay. Sermonettes for children are one of the favorite parts of the worship serice for me, and require at least as much thought as the sermon.

After telling stories for several years, friends suggested I write some of them down to share. I finally agreed. But I am all for parents and children communicating, discussing, learning and growing together. So I decided not to write a children's book. I wrote a series of lessons about symbols and missions that parents, grandparents, aunts, uncles, friends and pastors can share with children.

Hopefully, both adults and children will learn about the symbols we use and about the flow of the church year. These sermonettes follow the church year and I trust will make the church year a meaningful part of a child's Christian education. The church year is a marvelous tool to help us flow through the life, death and resurrection of Jesus each year.

D. Douglas Schneider
World Peace University
Portland, Oregon

ACKNOWLEDGEMENTS

There are several people I want to thank for encouragement in writing this book.

First, I thank the congregations at St. John's United Church of Christ, Marine City, Michigan; St. Paul's United Church of Christ, Grand Haven, Michigan; Waihee Protestant Church, Wailuku and Keawalai Congregational Church, Makena, Maui, Hawaii. Each of these congregations helped me to grow spiritually.

I thank Marylin Ordonēz-Schneider for her understanding and love during my writing.

Thanks to Monica Burnett for typing the final manuscript, and to my nephew, David Schneider for proof reading.

I thank my wife, Susan, who made the publishing of this book possible.

Special thanks go to my daughter, Kathleen Schneider, for asking many questions and for keeping me open and honest. Without her questioning, this book would not be.

D. Douglas Schneider

Special thanks go to Clifford Holbrook who provided the art work in this book and to Becky LaMothe for the cover design.

DEDICATION

This book is dedicated to my Mother:
Evelyn Bernice Schneider.

TABLE OF CONTENTS

Part II — CHURCH DAYS

Part III — SPECIAL DAYS

PART I

SUNDAYS IN THE CHURCH YEAR

1st Sunday In Advent

"WHAT IS ADVENT?"

Today is the first Sunday in Advent, and the beginning of the Christian Year. "Advent" means "arrival" and is the season of preparation for Christmas. Today is four Sundays before Christmas. We can use this Advent season to prepare our hearts and minds for the Christ child of Christmas. At Christmas we celebrate not only the birth of Jesus, but we celebrate the final coming.

Christmas was not celebrated until the fourth century A.D. because the Early Church looked to Easter first and only later began to look back at the birth of Jesus. They gave their attention to Easter first because there were so many troubles for them that they thought they might not be around in later years.

Because we have four Sundays before Christmas in Advent, we have four candles in the outside circle of the Advent wreath. The pink candle in the middle is a symbol of the Christ child. We'll light it on Christmas Eve.

Did you notice that our church colors changed today? The color has been green since last summer. Now we use purple or violet as the color of the Advent season. It symbolizes love and truth. It also symbolizes royalty: a king. Who is the king? Yes Jesus is the king whose birthday we celebrate.

Let us all use the things we do and think about between now and Christmas to prepare us for celebrating the birth of Jesus.

2nd Sunday In Advent

"THE CHRISTMAS TREE"

Some of you will help your family pick out a Christmas tree soon. Let us, today, look at the Christmas tree as a symbol of Christmas. Several countries have different stories about the Christmas tree. I will share one story.

We can trace the use of the Christmas tree by Christians back to the 16th century. But evergreen trees were used long before that as a symbol of immortality because evergreen stays green year round. Some people agree that Martin Luther put the first candles on the tree. Because people liked the idea, the custom spread throughout Europe.

The Christmas tree was probably brought to America by German immigrants. In Cleveland, Ohio, in 1851, a young pastor set up a lighted tree in church. The people got angry about it until he was able to prove that other Christians were using Christmas trees to celebrate Christmas.

It was not until 1918 that a Christmas tree was decorated outdoors. That happened in Denver, Colorado, where the custom soon became very popular.

Because the Christmas tree had many meanings from long ago, Christian symbols began to be used as decorations. These included angels, the stars and finally lights (now electric lights). Next week we will talk about the symbols of some of the decorations on the Christmas tree.

3

3rd Sunday in Advent

"TREE DECORATIONS"

Today is the third Sunday in Advent, which means we have one more Sunday before Christmas. I promised that I would talk to you about some of the symbols of the decorations we put on the Christmas tree. We use these decorations to remind us what Christmas is really all about.

The angels we may find on the Christmas tree stand for the angels of heaven who sang with the shepherds at the birth of Jesus.

The star stands for the star that stopped over the stable where the Christ child was born.

Tinsel and icicles were originally put on the Christmas tree as symbols of the hair of Jesus. Some people will remember "angels' hair" which was put on the tree to remind us of the angels.

Candles and later lights were put on the tree to remind us that Jesus is the light of the world.

Colored bulbs were originally put on the tree to remind us of the presents that were brought to the baby Jesus by the wise men. By the way, how many wise men were there? We don't know! The Bible story doesn't tell us. We are only told that three gifts were brought.

The Candy Cane

4th Sunday In Advent

"THE CANDY CANE"

The shepherds' staff was carried by shepherds when they went to visit the baby Jesus on the first Christmas morning. What do we use to remind us of the shepherds' first visit? The answer is: the candy cane.

The candy cane is such an old symbol that we have almost forgotten its origin. The colors of the candy cane are not by accident either. The red stripe was put in the candy cane to remind us of Jesus' sacrifice of himself for us. White is the symbol of Jesus' purity. The body of the candy cane is also white, representing the life that was pure.

The form of the candy cane, the shepherd's staff, suggests service — the gentle savior seeing that we all find God.

The smell of peppermint reminds us of the herb hyssop with its nice smell. Old Testament scholars tell us that hyssop not only tastes good, but was also used for medical purposes.

The candy cane is often broken in pieces for all to share, drawing us into a fellowship of sharing. From sharing we learn that we are all children of God and that as we give so we live.

Now when you look at a candy cane, my hope is that you will see more than a piece of candy, that you will also remember the rich symbols and what those symbols remind us about. They remind us about God and our relationship with Jesus.

1st Sunday After Christmas

"JESUS"

Wouldn't it be nice to know more about the boyhood of Jesus? It would be interesting to know more about Jesus' family and his younger brothers and sisters for whom he must have helped care. After the stories of the birth of Jesus there are several years of silence before he began his public ministry at Cana, where he and his mother went for a wedding.

If we had the stories about all the people Jesus helped in his 33 years on earth, it would be fascinating and the world's libraries would be enriched. But in Jesus' day books were rare and expensive because they were all written by hand. Each book was written on sheepskin or on handmade paper. The people who wrote the Gospels of Matthew, Mark, Luke and John had to be thrifty with their writing materials.

Teachers tell us that the first Gospel written was Mark and it was written about 30 years after Jesus died. Until the Gospel of Mark was written, the Good News was passed on by spoken word. As they grew old, the disciples and others realized that they needed to write the story of Jesus for future generations. They wanted the next generations, which include you and me, to know that God loves us without any conditions and that Jesus came to show us how to live.

We thank God for the birth stories of Jesus, and for the stories of his ministry.

2nd Sunday After Christmas

"MULTIPLICATION"

As we look into the New Year, it is helpful to realize that there is a multiplication of value by the presence of Jesus. Jesus' disciples were simple people. But when Jesus said "Follow me" and they accepted the invitation, they became people with power to begin a movement that has transformed or changed the world. That movement is the Church. And when we put Jesus ahead of ourselves in our lives, we too become someone of great worth.

An example is the zero. A zero means nothing by itself. But when you combine a zero with another number, it can have great value. If we take a zero and put a 1 before it, what do we have? The answer is 10. If we add only zeroes to zeroes, we still end up with nothing. But if we put a zero after 10, what do we get? 100!

If you think that this new year doesn't hold much for you, if you feel like a zero, put Jesus into your life and you will find that you have great value.

We can really make the new year a very good year for spiritual growth if we are willing to follow the law of multiplication: Jesus in your life can really help change the world and make it a better place for all of us to live in.

1st Sunday After Epiphany

"THE 12 DAYS OF CHRISTMAS"

(Suggestion: Sing part of "The 12 Days of Christmas")

We are in a new season of the Church year today. January 6 is Epiphany. The word Epiphany means "manifestation" or "revealing." There are 12 days between Christmas and Epiphany — that is where we get the song, "The 12 Days of Christmas."

January 6 is the anniversary of the night the Wise Men were guided to Bethlehem by the star. It marks the end of the Christmas season. The Wise Men recognized who Jesus was; therefore, we say that Jesus was revealed or made known to them, Epiphany is associated with the star that led the Wise Men. The Epiphany star is five-pointed. This star is the ancient symbol for the perfection of Man, or the perfection of Christ's life. Another symbol of Epiphany is the candle. How does the candle give us light? Answer: by burning itself up, by giving of itself. We use God's love by giving it away; that is, by being loving.

By the year 354 A.D. the birth of Jesus was already mentioned as December 25, and Epiphany was celebrated for a long time as the third most important holiday in the Church, after Easter and Pentecost. Then Christmas began to be celebrated as more important. The Epiphany season is the season of Jesus' light shining on us, revealing to us who Jesus was. This season lasts until the beginning of Lent, and the color for Epiphany is white.

The Epiphany season is a wonderful time of the year to learn what Jesus means to you and to me.

2nd Sunday After Epiphany

"BAPTISM"

In the Greek Church, Jesus' baptism is celebrated on January 6, so the Epiphany season has many symbols for us. Today we want to talk about the meaning of baptism.

Baptism is the ceremony by which a person becomes part of the Christian Church. When John the Baptist baptized Jesus, there was not yet a Christian Church. The Church came into being only after Jesus' death, but because of Jesus' baptism the early Church believed baptism was very important.

Some churches baptize infants. At that time the parents and the church both make a promise to provide the kind of upbringing in which the child can learn about God's love and make his or her own decision to become a Christian. Confirmation is a time of confirming the decision of the parents for persons baptized as infants. Some churches baptize only adults, waiting for the person to become old enough to make his or her own decision about God and Jesus.

A person's name, in years past and still today in some parts of the world, was given at baptism. We call that name "the Christian name."

We know that all people are created by God and that we all belong to God. Baptism is our recognition that we belong to God and are called "Children of God."

3rd Sunday After Epiphany

"A LESSON IN A BEE STING"

Buzz! Buzz! The bees were flying around the hive excitedly. One of the children from the visiting Sunday School had hit a bee hive with a stone as they walked through the orchard. The children started to run, but Patty was stung. The teacher took the children into the beekeeper's house and put some medicine on Patty's sting.

"Ouch, it hurts!" cried Patty.

"Yes, it does hurt, and I'm sorry," replied the teacher. "But you know, the bee stung you only to protect the other bees. Bees generally have a reason for stinging people."

The beekeeper added, "The bee that stung you was probably a guard bee and died soon after she stung you. When a bee stings, she is seriously injured while trying to pull the stinger out. She dies to protect the hive."

The teacher asked, "Please tell us some more about bees."

The beekeeper answered, "Bees are some of the most

fascinating creatures in the world. In one bee hive there can be as many as 60,000 bees and only one queen. All the worker bees are female."

"Wow," exclaimed John. "That is a lot of bees."

The beekeeper went on, "Yes it is. When lots of food is available from flowers, the queen bee lays more eggs to produce more bees to bring in more food. When the bees are very busy during the summer they live only about 3 weeks."

Patty asked, "Do all bees work?"

"All bees work except the drones, who are the males. And there are never many of them. But all bees do not do the same work. You were stung by a guard bee. It is their job to protect the hive from danger."

"What other kinds of bees are there?" asked John.

"Well, there are bees who collect the nectar and pollen from the flowers. There are also bees who keep the hive clean and others who feed the young."

"So all the bees work together then," suggested Patty.

The teacher answered, "Yes, bees work together to help the colony live. It is a shame that people are not more like bees in being willing to cooperate together to do things."

The beekeeper declared, "Yes, if each person did his or her part, the world would be a much nicer place in which to live."

The teacher added, "That is what God wants us to do: to work together. We can learn from bees about how God wants us to cooperate with each other."

"Yes," Patty whispered. "And I also learned that a bee does not sting people without a reason."

"HELPING HANDS"

During a hike in the woods a Girl Scout Troop came across an abandoned section of railroad track. The girls tried to walk the rails but each soon fell off.

Suddenly two girls boasted that they could both walk the entire track without falling off. They were challenged to "put up or shut up." The two girls jumped up on opposite rails, extended a hand to balance each other, and walked a section of track without falling off because they were supporting each other.

We do things better and we live better by helping each other. The person who helps, helps both himself or herself and the other person. When there is no cooperation and no spirit of helping, what could be pleasant jobs become tedious or grudging chores.

What is the Golden Rule? Answer: Do unto others as you would have them do unto you. This same Golden Rule is found in all 7 great religions:

Hindu: The true rule is to guard and do by the things of others as you would by your own.

Buddhist: One should seek for others the happiness one desires for oneself.

Zoroastrian: Do as you would be done by.

Confucian: What you do not wish done to you, do not to others.

Moslem: Let none of you treat your brother in a way he himself would dislike to be treated.

Jewish: Whatever you do not wish of your neighbor to do to you, do not unto him.

Christian: All things whatsoever ye would that men should do unto you, do even so to them.

5th Sunday After Epiphany

"SUNDAY"

Today is Sunday, the first day of the week. Before Jesus was born, the Jews celebrated, and they still do, the Jewish Sabbath, which is now on Saturday.

After the death of Jesus, His disciples and friends began to celebrate Sunday as the weekly memorial of Easter. Matthew tells us that Mary Magdalene went to Jesus' grave "the first day of the week." The celebration of the Resurrection took place on that Sunday when the disciples met together and Jesus showed himself to them again. The author of the Book of Revelation gave the day its name, "The Lord's Day," in Revelation 1:10.

Sunday, then, each Sunday, is a celebration of the first Easter and the Resurrection of Jesus. It is also a day of hope and anticipation of the return of Christ.

In the early Roman Empire, Sunday was not only a day of joyful worship but also a work day. The Roman ruler Constantine I made Sunday into a day of rest in the year 321 A.D.

Not all countries in the world celebrate Sunday as a day of rest. Some countries where Islam is the main religion celebrate Friday as their worship and rest day, and Israel celebrates Saturday as its Jewish Sabbath.

For Christians, Sunday is a very special day on which we remember the first Easter and think about God's great love for us, a love that has no conditions upon it.

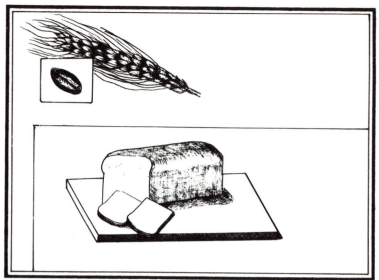

6th Sunday After Epiphany
"BREAD"

We use bread in our Communion services as a symbol of the body of Jesus, given to us so that we might know God more completely and be able to respond to God's love. Bread is also important to life.

How long does it take to bake a loaf of bread? Answer: 6 months. Why does it take that long? The wheat has to be planted, first, then it has to be fertilized. Once ripe it has to be harvested. But still it isn't ready to be made into bread. It must be milled. Then it has to be sold and someone has to buy it. It takes all that before wheat is ready to be made into bread. That is why I answered that it takes 6 months to bake a loaf of bread.

How long does it take a person to grow into a loving relationship with God? Answer: a lifetime. That is one project we want to work on throughout our entire lives.

Some lifetimes are shorter than others, but the whole time that a person lives, she or he is growing spiritually. Growing in an awareness of how much God loves us does not stop, but is something we need to keep doing all the time.

It takes only a few minutes to bake a loaf of bread once we have the wheat grown, harvested, milled and made into flour. It takes only a few minutes to say "Yes" to Jesus once we have spent the time feeling God's love working in our lives.

7th Sunday After Epiphany

"THE RAINBOW"

From Genesis 9:13-14 we know that the rainbow is a very old symbol to remind people of God's promises. For example, the promise to bring everybody's life into the beauty of the rainbow. In fact today, for fun, we say that there must be a pot of gold at the end of the rainbow. We say that because the rainbow reminds us of how faithful God is.

A rainbow is really a circle of color. It is colored light caused when the sun strikes falling raindrops. Rainbows are curved because the raindrops that reflect the light are curved. Each raindrop bends and separates sunlight into bands of distinct colors, just as a prism does.

Primary rainbows are what we usually see. The primary rainbow's colors are arranged in the order of the color spectrum: the outside is red, then orange, yellow, green and blue or violet. Secondary rainbow colors are reversed. The secondary rainbow is the second and fainter of the rainbows we see if we are lucky enough to see two at one time.

In many rainbows one or more of the colors may drop out. Often the blue will not be in a rainbow, but red is almost always present. The next time you see a rainbow, look carefully and notice the colors to see if they are all present. There are no rainbows if the sun is at an altitude of over 42 degrees; that is why we don't see rainbows at noon.

We thank God for the beautiful rainbows we see, and we thank God for the wonderful promises made to us.

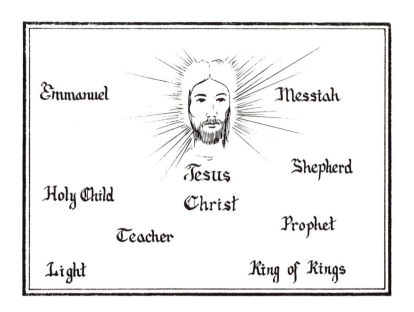

Emmanuel Messiah Holy Child Jesus Christ Shepherd Teacher Prophet Light King of Kings

8th Sunday After Epiphany

"NAMES FOR JESUS"

Names are something we all have. They help us identify who we are. Most names have a meaning. Here are some examples:

Douglas means "dark water," Mary is Greek for "a sea of bitterness or sorrow," Marilyn means a descendant of Mary. Kathleen is a spelling for Cathleen and means "pure"; Karen is a variant of Cathleen. David is Hebrew for "beloved." Delano is Old French and means "of the night," Ben is a Hebrew name meaning "son of my right hand." Ken is Scottish meaning "handsome." Jack is from the Hebrew "Jacob" meaning "held by the heel or supplanter." Janice, Jane, Janet and Janis are the feminine form of John, meaning "gracious or merciful." Judy is from the Hebrew word meaning "praise" and Diane is Latin for "bright, pure as day." Lloyd is from a Welsh word meaning grey or brown, and Ruth comes from Hebrew for "friendship." Richard comes from Teutonic and means "powerful" or "treasurer of the kingdom." Franklin is Old English for "free-holder" and Bernice is Greek for "bringer of victory." Evelyn is Celtic for "pleasant."

In the King James Version of the Bible there are 144 names for Jesus. Some of the common names for Jesus are: Jesus, Emmanuel, First Begotten, Friend of Sinners, Holy Child, Messiah, Shepherd, Teacher, Christ, Prophet and Light.

Some names for Jesus that are not so common: Amen (Revelation 3:14), Angel (Malachi 3:1), Bishop (I Peter 2:25), Captain (Hebrews 2:10), Judge (Acts 10:42), Lion (Revelation 5:5), Morning Star (Revelation 2:28) and Prince (Acts 3:15).

Whatever name we use for Jesus, we can be sure of one thing: Jesus loves each one of us without any conditions.

9th Sunday After Epiphany

"NAMES FOR THE CHURCH"

Last Sunday we discussed the different names we find in the Bible for Jesus. How many are there in the King James Version? Answer: 144.

We also discussed our own names and how important they are to us and the fact that almost all names have a meaning.

Today we want to think about names for the Church. How many names for the Church do we find in the King James Version of the Bible? 109

Some of them are:

Christians   (Acts 11:20 and I Peter 4:16)
Wise Men   (I Corinthians 6:5)
Woman   (Revelation 12:1)
Stones   (I Peter 2:5)
Family of God
House of God
Angels
Believers
Body of Christ
Bride
Children of the Kingdom
Jacob
Jewels of the Lord
Palm Tree
Sheep

Whatever the name we use for the Church, the Church is a wonderful place to spend Sunday morning and other times during the week.

10th Sunday After Epiphany

"WHEN SOMEONE DIES"

Death is a subject many people don't like to talk about or think about. But if we can't talk about death in church, where can we talk about it?

God is a God of love. The Bible tells us that we are all "children of God." God really cares for and loves each of us as individuals.

God does not "call us home" to heaven. We go to heaven, yes, but we were created here to grow to be spiritual persons, and God doesn't get lonely for us and call us there. In fact, God can be with us as much now as in heaven, if we allow that to happen, because God is both fully in heaven and fully here and now.

God is sorrowful when someone dies because there is hurt, loss and pain associated with death. God weeps because we weep and that shows how much God cares for us. However, God sees death differently than most of us do. Death is a door to another life, a life in which we no longer have the limitations of our physical bodies as we do now. In God's view, death is not an enemy to be conquered but a door to go through. Yes, for most of us it is painful to go through that door. We don't like to give up the physical presence of our loved ones and friends.

Praise God that through Jesus we know of the next life, and praise God for helping us to let go of this life when the time comes to do so.

1st Sunday In Lent

"LENT"

The word "Lent" comes from a word which means "lengthening of days." The days during this season are getting longer as we get closer to spring.

There are 46 days during the Lenten season, but there are only 40 days in Lent. We do not count Sundays or observe Lent on Sundays, because Sundays are set aside for the celebration of the Resurrection of Jesus.

The number 40 is used many times in the Bible, in reference to Moses, Elijah and Jesus. Remember how many days Jesus spent in the wilderness? Answer: 40.

Do you know about the Mardi Gras celebration in New Orleans and other places? That is connected with Lent. Mardi Gras means "fat Tuesday." It comes the day before Ash Wednesday, which is the first day of Lent. Mardi Gras is the last day of eating and drinking too much before Lent, when many people try to be careful about eating and drinking too much. In fact, some people "give up" something during Lent as a sign that they are thinking about what Jesus did for us on Good Friday. It is a good time to give up bad habits and to make a special effort to be what God created us to be: loving persons. We can use Lent as a time to prepare our hearts to receive the Risen Lord of Easter morning.

The color for the Lenten season is purple or violet, as a sign of feeling sorry for the bad things we have done. Not only feeling sorry, but changing our ways so that we do only loving things.

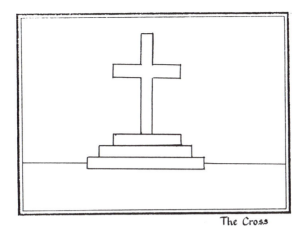

The Cross

2nd Sunday In Lent

"THE CROSS"

Of all the Christian symbols today, the cross is the most universally used and accepted. There are more than 400 various shapes of the cross in existence.

Strange as it may seem, the cross wasn't used as widely much before the 5th century. As early as the 2nd century, Christians were signing themselves with veiled crosses as a secret mark of identification. The most common of those was the anchor. But the cross was not used as we use it until much later. When Spaniards took possession of Central America, they found in native temples crosses, which were regarded as a symbol of divinity. They concluded the cross must have reached America through Christian missions of which all traces were lost. But certainly that was not the case. The cross before Columbus came to America was a kind of compass that represented the four quarters of the earth.

The most popular form of all crosses is the Latin cross, the form on which it is said Jesus was crucified. When the Latin cross stands on three steps it is called the Calvary cross. The steps signify faith, hope and love, and the cross itself symbolized the finished work of the risen Christ.

Occasionally in Protestant Churches and in most Roman Catholic Churches the figure of Christ is on the cross, which is

21

then called a crucifix. The crucifix is a symbol of the Lord's passion and atonement.

Many of the 400 shapes of the cross convey no symbolic idea but were mere heraldic devices, interesting now only for decoration. The cross, in whatever form, is a symbol of the Christian faith, the love of God for all people, and the triumphant hope.

3rd Sunday In Lent

"THE THANK YOU HOUSE"

During the Lenten Season we like to think about the needs of others. In the church we call that "missions." Almost every church spends money and sends money for mission programs around the world.

We sometimes hear suggestions that people do not appreciate what we do for them. Let us report here that this is not true. We are not only appreciated, but our giving gives us a chance to feel part of the World Family of God.

Let me tell you a story of being thankful. In a little village in the jungles of Orissa, India, a mission program helped to save a village from a forest fire and helped them grow more food. Then a famine came along. There was no rain for one year and the people couldn't grow their usual rice crop. They had nothing to eat. The mission program provided food for that village so that the people could build a dam. The dam would store water once it rained and the people in the meantime could have food.

After the famine the people called the missionary to the village. They had a surprise. The village leader said to the missionary, "Our Christian brothers and sisters sent us food when we were starving. We want to thank all of them through you. Here is a house for you in our village. We built it ourselves and we give it to you. It is a 'thank you' to all those who gave so that we could eat when we were hungry."

That "Thank You" house is now used as a church.

"KUMARI"

Last Sunday we talked about a "thank you" house. Today we want to talk about one little girl in that village in India.

Do you like school? Would you like to walk 2½ miles through jungle one way to school every day? That is what 8-year-old Kumari had to do. She liked school that much, but she wanted more. Kumari wanted to go to the mission school 100 miles away. But how? Her family had no money. Kumari knew that she could learn more in the mission school. Her village had no TV, no radio, no newspaper and only a few books. Kumari had never been further away from home than her school 2½ miles away.

A missionary visited her small village and talked to the people. He talked to Kumari. He could tell that she was very smart. Because people in churches in the United States had given money to mission programs, the missionary could say to Kumari, "Yes, you can go to mission school!"

Do you know how much it cost each month for Kumari to stay at the mission school? $10.00, which included her food, school books and supplies and clothes.

That is how some of our mission money is used, to help people like Kumari. Kumari studied hard, became a nurse, and now she is able to work in a mission hospital to help others.

5th Sunday In Lent

"THE BUTTERFLY"

The early Church used the butterfly as a symbol for Jesus' Resurrection. In its transforming cycle, a butterfly goes from a lowly caterpillar to a cocoon and finally grows into a beautiful butterfly, a symbol of God's promise of victory over the grave.

There are nearly 20,000 kinds of butterflies. The largest butterfly is the Queen Alexandra Birdwing of New Guinea. It has a wing span of eleven inches. The smallest butterfly is the Western Pygmy Blue of North America with a wingspan of only three-eighths of an inch.

Butterflies begin as tiny eggs that hatch into caterpillars. The caterpillars eat and grow, shedding their skin as they grow. Finally the caterpillars form a protective shell called a cocoon. Inside the cocoons the worms change into beautiful butterflies.

Most butterflies live only a week or two, but a few kinds will live up to 18 months. Butterflies eat nectar from flowers.

The butterfly, because of its stages of development and beauty, is a wonderful symbol to think about. We are reminded by the butterfly that there is life after this life, and the next life will be one of beauty and love. God promises us that the grave is not our last stop. Our souls live on and will continue to be in communion with God.

6th Sunday In Lent

"PALM TREES"

The word "palm" comes from the Latin word "palma" which means both the hand and a tree, because the leaf of a palm tree looks much like a human hand.

There are more than 100 species of palm trees, but the ones found in Palestine where Jesus grew up are the date palm. The date palm grows to heights of 50 to 90 feet. The female tree bears a cluster of up to 200 dates. The tree may bear fruit for over 200 years. The dates from the date palm are 50 percent sugar, and in times of no rain they become a main energy-producing crop in Arabia and Africa.

The palm tree came to be regarded as a symbol of victory and triumph. On the very first Palm Sunday, people took palm branches and waved them as a sign that the event would lead to victory. But Jesus' triumphal entry into the city of Jerusalem was misunderstood by those who wanted a political leader who would throw the Roman rulers out of their country.

What the people got was a victory for all of us — the victory of the cross, the victory over the grave. Today we still use palm branches as a symbol of Jesus' victory which he gives to each of us.

Easter Sunday

"EASTER EGGS"

The name Easter is of uncertain origin but may have come from the Anglo-Saxon spring goddess "Eostre" who represented light and spring, therefore Easter. The time of Easter is the beginning of spring, and spring is an important season in all religions.

Eggs had been used as symbols of new life and resurrection long before the first Easter. In many places decorated eggs were presented as tokens of wishes for a long life and good fortune.

The Easter rabbit originally had nothing to do with Easter either. The rabbit is a symbol that the land will grow good crops. There is a story of a noblewoman who escaped from one of the wars in Europe by hiding in the mountains. Because eggs were unknown by the mountain people, she ordered her servants to get some from the town nearby. She had the eggs colored and asked the children to build nests in the forest. The servants put eggs in the nests and when the children found them the next day, they believed Easter bunnies brought them. That is one story that tries to explain why Easter bunnies and Easter eggs are associated. It was not until the Civil War that the Easter customs of rabbits and eggs came to the U.S.A.

The Emperor Constantine started the custom of new Easter clothes. He told his court members to appear Easter morning in new clothes and they did. Since then it has become a custom to wear new clothing on Easter day.

26

At Easter in many churches white lilies are put in front as a symbol of light and purity.

But it is more important how we live than what symbols we use for Easter. The real symbols of Easter are being forgiving, loving, caring and joyful.

2nd Sunday Of Easter

"FIRE AND ELEPHANTS"

We can do great things, sometimes even surprising things, if we allow God to help us. God can help us by giving us courage and strength to meet the demands made upon us. I want to tell you a story about an Indian village and how it was saved by prayer and work.

The small village of Sikuli is located on a mountain in the jungles of India. When it rains there it really rains, but when it stops raining it may not rain again for six months. One dry season a forest fire broke out near the village. The villagers did not think much about it because every dry season forest fires burn near the village. However, this time the winds were quite high and the village soon was surrounded on three sides by fire. The fire was very hot and dangerous to the people because their houses were made of mud and bamboo with grass roofs.

The villagers feared it would not be long before the whole village would catch on fire. They decided to carry off a few things and run away from the fire. They gathered together and began to move out. The younger boys ran ahead to make sure the fire had not spread across their path of escape.

About 100 yards from the village the boys came unexpectedly across a herd of elephants. They ran back to warn the others that the elephants were blocking the path of escape and that the elephants were not happy with the fire either. The villagers were as afraid of the elephants as they were of the fire. They returned to the village and held a prayer meeting on the spot. Each person got down on his or her knees and asked God for courage and strength to save themselves. The village headman finally arose and said, "We must save the village to save ourselves. If we run away and our village is destroyed, we shall have nothing. God will give us strength."

They formed a bucket brigade from the village well to the houses and wet down the grass roofs. This was not easy because there were only a few buckets. Some of the men took shovels and made a fire break, clearing the dry grass away from around the village.

The fire swept past the village and across the escape route but the village was safe. As the fire swept by, the elephants became frightened and ran away. The people were saved from both the fire and the elephants.

The villagers showed that God can and does give us courage and strength, if we ask help in times of trouble. We can do even more than our own capabilities if we rely upon God to add grace to what we can do ourselves. God helps those who help themselves and who call upon God when they reach the limit of helping themselves. God never abandons us.

3rd Sunday Of Easter

"THE LAW"

"You shall love the Lord your God with all your heart, soul and mind." (Deuteronomy 6:5) "You shall love your neighbor as yourself." (Luke 19:18) These two scripture passages are the summary of the law.

In Jesus' day there were 613 commandments. Of those, 365 were negative: they told you what you could not do. There were 248 positive commandments of the Jewish Law.

Jesus took all of them into consideration and reduced them to the two we began with: Love God, and love your neighbor as yourself. We are called to be true to our highest self, which is the self in God. We strive to love God the way we want our neighbor to love us.

As God has loved us in Jesus, so we can honor our own

lives. We know that we are dear to God. In that awareness we can love ourselves, and love our neighbors as much.

God does not require us to compare ourselves to others. God wants each of us to be what we are: unique individuals. We are able to accept ourselves, to understand ourselves, not because we obey all the laws — because we know we don't, but because we know that we are loved and accepted by God and Jesus.

Nothing can be more deep or more real or ultimately more satisfying than to feel and know the acceptance we have from God as we experience such acceptance in Jesus.

4th Sunday Of Easter

"OBEY YOUR PARENTS"

Today I want to talk about obeying your parents. They may not always give you a good reason for what they ask you to do, but they generally **have** a very good reason for what they tell you.

In a small town in Michigan a pastor went to visit a hospital one evening. He was shocked! In that evening three children were brought in for emergency treatment. One child had a bean in his ear. The second child had a broken jaw from being hit by the bat when he got too close to the plate while playing baseball. The third boy had a broken arm. He had run into a fence. Why were those three children in one small hospital the same evening?

Part of the answer is that they did not do as their parents asked. I know that you like your parents to explain things to you and they do not always do that. But you can be sure that they love you and want the best for you. Obeying your parents will help you keep out of trouble.

Remember, please: your parents love you and God loves you. Your first experience of God's love is through the love of your parents.

5th Sunday Of Easter

"LOCKS"

(Note to reader: Have a couple locks with keys and combinations.)

In school do you have locks on your locker? Do you have locks on the doors of your home? What if you forget the combination or the key to the lock? You would have a hard time getting in, wouldn't you?

Let us pretend something. Suppose you or a younger brother or sister gets locked in the bathroom from the inside. What would you do to get out? Well, some locks are made with special keys to open the lock from the other side. But sometimes the door has to be taken off.

What is the combination or lock to our hearts? Sometimes we feel bad. Our parents or brothers or sisters try to help, but we still don't feel right. Our friends try to help but fail.

A key or combination to our feeling bad can be prayer. Yes, prayer. When we ask God to help us we often begin to feel better very soon. One reason for this is that sometimes we feel bad because events are happening in our lives over which we seem to have no control. And we like to be in control, don't we? So when we are not in control, we don't feel so good in our hearts. But if we give God a chance to be in control of our lives, suddenly we feel a lot better.

God knows the combination to your heart.

6th Sunday Of Easter

"A GLASS OF WATER"

(Note to reader: Use a glass of water as a teaching aid.)

Water is essential to life. No one can live more than three days without water. Yet most of us take water for granted. We turn the faucet on and expect to have water come out. We keep the faucet on and waste water.

In many places in the world, water is hard to get and is not taken for granted. In fact for many people, water is considered a gift of God. That is a very healthy way to think about water. In many parts of the world a person can stop and ask for water nearly anyplace, and water will be given freely. For physical life, water is essential.

In our spiritual lives, what is essential? The single most important ingredient to our spiritual lives, after faith is prayer. Without prayer we have no way to reach the source of our very being — our spiritual selves, our souls.

Prayer keeps us spiritually alive. Prayer keeps us in contact with God. With water and prayer we feed our whole selves, both body and soul.

7th Sunday Of Easter

"THE FALLING TREE"

Billy and Mary were hiking in the woods with their parents when a sudden spring storm came up. They dashed under a large bush near the edge of the woods for some shelter from the hard-hitting rain drops. As they watched the storm cross the open field in front of them they noticed the wind blowing very hard. One lone tree in the field stood against the fury of the storm. Suddenly they heard a sharp crack and saw the tree waving in the wind. Slowly the tree fell over with a thud.

"Wow!" cried Billy. "That tree really went crash."

"Yes," replied Mary, "The wind sure was strong."

Father answered, "That is one of the problems of one tree standing alone. When a big storm comes along the tree has to take the full wind all by itself."

Mother added, "One tree alone doesn't have much chance in a very bad storm. The redwood trees of California are an example of trees that stand together. Some of them grow as high as 300 feet and as large as 15 to 20 feet in diameter."

"That sounds like a huge tree," said astonished Mary.

31

"It is a huge tree," replied father. "Moreover, the bark can be 12 inches thick and the rings of one tree proved that the tree was at least 4000 years old before it fell down."

"What is the largest redwood tree?" asked Billy?

Father answered, "The tree considered the largest redwood tree is called the General Sherman Tree. It is almost 300 feet high and weighs 6,167 tons. It has enough wood in it to build more than 20 average size houses. Some other redwoods are higher but not as heavy."

"Why don't such huge trees fall down in a wind storm?" asked Mary.

Father replied, "That is an interesting question. The redwood trees grow in groves or groups. The roots of the redwood are shallow but because the trees grow near one another, their roots support each other and they are strong enough as a group to resist the winds. A single redwood growing alone wouldn't have much chance in a storm and would never grow very high before it was blown down."

Mother added, "People are also like that. Those people who stand alone get pushed around in this world. People who work together in groups and stand together help each other and the troubles of the world don't push them over. I believe that in God's plan for us, we are to learn to work together as God's children so that when trouble comes we can support and help each other. How wonderful it would be if the whole world of people were one big family working together."

Pentecost

"PENTECOST"

In the days when Jesus was growing up, on the morning of the second day of Passover, the community took a measure of barley to the temple. Surely Jesus did the same. Barley was one of the first grain crops to ripen in the spring. Wheat started ripening seven weeks later, so there were 50 days between barley ripening and wheat ripening. Those 50 days were called "Counting of the measure."

On the 50th day, the Jewish nation celebrated the summer festival "Shavuous." Many people would go to Jerusalem to the temple to give the first fruits of their fields and orchards for their offering.

"Shavuous" is the Hebrew word for seven weeks. Pentecost is the Greek word for the 50th day, and Pentecost comes fifty days after Easter.

Pentecost is considered by many to be the birthday of the Christian Church. Because it is a festival, the color we use and wear is red. We can read the story of the first Pentecost in Acts 2:1-4. The story tells us that a group of people were gathered together and that they were filled with the Holy Spirit.

Pentecost is also called "Whitsunday" or White Sunday because in the early Church, the persons to be baptized on Pentecost wore white baptismal robes.

Let us all sing "Happy Birthday" to the Church.

1st Sunday After Pentecost

"TRINITY SUNDAY"

Today is Trinity Sunday, the Sunday after Pentecost, which was the birthday of the Christian Church. The Trinity Season is the longest season of the Church year. It can have a maximum of 27 weeks or as few as 23 weeks. We focus on teachings about Jesus during this season, which lasts from today until Advent begins, four Sundays before Christmas.

Trinity Sunday was introduced by Pope John XXII, who was pope between 1316 and 1334. He introduced Trinity Sunday to honor the "Trinity": Father, Son and Holy Spirit.

We do not worship three gods, but One God. We do, however, relate to God in three ways: God as creator, God as sustainer, and God with us. These three ways of relating to God are explained by the Trinity. It is something like the same person being in different relationships at the same time. The same person can be a father, a son, an uncle and a grandfather. This doesn't cut the person up in pieces; we simply use different words to explain these different relationships.

That is what the Trinity is all about: explaining the different relationships we have with God. We worship a single God who relates to us in different ways.

The color for this season is green, the color of growth.

"DR. CHARLES DREW"

More than 45 years ago a brilliant young doctor named Charles Drew discovered the use of blood plasma in saving human lives. Millions of people have been saved, especially during wars, by the use of blood plasma where whole blood is not available.

Charles Drew became Director of the National Blood Bank Program and also taught at Howard Medical School. He was a great teacher and a warm human being.

On April 1, 1950, Dr. Drew, with some other doctors, was driving to a medical conference and had an automobile accident in North Carolina. Dr. Drew was taken to the nearest hospital badly injured. The hospital denied him treatment because of the color of his skin. He was black.

He had to be taken to another hospital that would accept blacks. Dr. Drew died on the way to that other hospital. Isn't that sad — a wonderful man who had helped so many people live with his medical discovery was denied hospital treatment because of the color of his skin?

What kind of world do we live in that allows such a thing to happen? Certainly the love Jesus proclaimed and which we accept isn't consistent with such happenings. Jesus died for **all** people. There are no exceptions.

We can thank the Lord that such barriers have been broken down so that people are no longer denied hospital treatment because of the color of their skin. We thank God for the life of Dr. Charles Drew and the gift of blood plasma which he gave to the world.

3rd Sunday After Pentecost

"THE SHORTEST PRAYER"

We are great for shortening words. One example is "O.K." How much shorter a word can you get than that!

O.K. was first used in the name of the Democratic O.K. Club, in which O.K. was the abbreviation of "Old Kinderhook," the hometown of President Martin Van Buren, whom the club supported for a second term as president in 1840.

The shortest and most common prayer we say is "Goodbye." How many of you know that "Goodbye" is a prayer? Spoken in full, it once was, "God be with you."

In church, the prayer called the benediction at the end of the worship service is a goodbye from the minister to the congregation until they come together again for worship.

The French word "Adieu" comes from a word that means "I commend you to God" and is also used like "goodbye." "Adios" in Spanish means "Go with God."

While we don't think of "Goodbye" as a prayer, it really is one. It is a very nice way to leave someone: with the thought of God being with that other person.

4th Sunday After Pentecost

"JESUS' TEACHINGS"

Do you know what the main idea in Jesus' teachings was?

After Jesus' death, his friends and disciples got together and formed a community. They tried to live the main teaching Jesus gave them. That main idea was LOVE. Jesus told them that the most important thing they could do was to love God and to love their neighbors as themselves.

You and I are transmitters of God's love. In one sense, we are God's broadcasting stations. When we are on the right frequency, we receive God's love and then send it on to those around us.

In amateur radio there are "repeaters," which are stations set up to send messages on from small stations so that the messages can go much further. There are thousands of repeaters all over the United States of America. Most of the repeaters are privately owned — they are put up by someone to use and for the use of anyone needing a repeater. Some repeaters are fixed in such a way that you can call a phone number through them.

We receive very strong signals from God. God really does love us. How strong are the signals we send? How good repeaters are we? If we are not sending out strong LOVE signals, maybe we need to take a look at what we are doing, because the message God gives us to send is LOVE.

5th Sunday After Pentecost

"ECOLOGY"

What is the meaning of "ecology"? We hear the word used a lot nowadays, but what does it mean? Ecology deals with relations between living things and their environment. We live on this planet and all life — plants, water, soil and other things — is part of our environment.

The Christian counterpart or word for "ecology" is "stewardship." Good stewardship means taking care of this world God has given us to enjoy and use for our needs. Stewardship also means sharing what we have.

In a real sense, the land, water, trees and living things around us have only been lent to us by God to enjoy while we are here. God's plan is for us to take care of the world so that it can be passed on to those who follow. The best concern we can have for ecology is being good stewards.

The American Indian named Chief Seattle, in 1854 spoke to an assembly of tribes preparing to sign treaties. He said, "How can you buy or sell the sky, the warmth of the land? The idea is strange to us. If we do not own the freshness of the air and the sparkle of the water, how can you buy them? . .

"Every part of the earth is sacred to my people. Every shining pine needle, every sandy shore, every mist in the dark woods, every humming insect is holy in the memory and experience of my people . . .

"The earth does not belong to man: man belongs to the earth. This we know. All things are connected like blood which unites one family.

"Whatever befalls the earth befalls the sons of the earth. Man did not weave the web of life, he is merely a strand in it. Whatever he does to the web, he does to himself."

6th Sunday After Pentecost

"SUMMER"

What is summer? Summer is defined as the time of year when the sun is furthest from the equator, north, on June 21 or 22.

How quickly summer comes and goes. In some parts of the world the summers seem very short. In Barrow, Alaska, summer really starts in August and ends in September, but during that time there are 24 hours of daylight every day. Can you imagine all day and all night for one month without darkness? It is hard to sleep and people stay up very late. But they get their chance to sleep in the winter when they have a whole month with no sunlight!

We do want to thank God for the creation of this wonderful world with its different seasons. Today we can be thankful for summer which gives us time to enjoy being outside, to go on vacation maybe, to see things grow and then see them harvested. God really has been very good to us.

How thankful are you for what God has given you? How thankful are you for summer? Enjoy summer as a creation and wonder of our loving Creator God. For those of you going away for the summer, have a safe and wonderful summer, and may God bless you.

7th Sunday After Pentecost

"THE BIBLE"

The word "Bible" comes from the Greek "biblia" meaning books. The Protestant Bible is a collection of 66 writings. Catholic, Anglican and Eastern Orthodox Bibles contain 73 writings.

The Bible was written by many different authors over a period of more than 1000 years, from about 900 B.C. to 100 A.D. These writings are about God and God's relationship with people. God is telling us one message. What do you think that message is?

(Note: Have a piece of paper in an envelope in the Bible you are holding. Written on the paper are the words "I LOVE YOU.")

Let us think about the Bible as being a letter from God to you and me. Here is the letter. (Take the letter out of the Bible.) Let us see what God's message to us is. (Open the letter and read it.) "I love you." Isn't that a wonderful message? So we say that the Bible is a love letter from God to you and me and all the people in the world. It is a message we all need to hear.

In church we use an open Bible as a symbol of God's word of love to us. What a wonderful loving God we have. What can you and I give to such a wonderful God? Our own love.

We talked about the Bible and the fact that it has many different books in it. One book in the Bible does not mention God. Does anyone know what book that is? It is the Book of Esther. Esther is the story of a Jewish girl who became Queen of Persia and saved her people from destruction. There is no mention of God in the story, but God's love and caring for Esther and her family are very obvious in the Book of Esther.

8th Sunday After Pentecost

"HOW THE BIBLE DEVELOPED"

Last week we said that the Bible is a collection of writings about God and God's relationship with people. We also mentioned that the Bible is a love story or letter in which God says, "I love you and all the people of the world."

The Bible is divided into two parts; The old agreement and the new agreement. Agreement means "testament." The old agreement was between God and the Hebrews when the Hebrews left Egypt. The new agreement is between God and all people, based on the teachings and life of Jesus.

The Bible was written by many different people in several languages in several places, over a period of 1000 years. After much discussion the individual books were finally gathered together into the book we now call the "Holy Bible."

In 98 A.D. a committee of Jewish teachers determined or decided which would be the books of the Old Testament, based on three things: (1) that they were written before 400 B.C., (2) that they were written in the Hebrew language, and (3) that they had moral character.

In 393 A.D. a church council acknowledged many of the books in the New Testament as inspired and special. Later, Anthanasius, who was Bishop of Alexandria, made a list of the books which we have in the New Testament today, and that list became accepted by most Christians.

However the Bible came to us, we want to thank God for such a wonderful letter to us.

"THE FOUR GOSPELS"

The word "Gospel" means "good news." There are four books in the Bible that we call the Gospels. What are they? Matthew, Mark, Luke and John.

Some people get confused when they read the Gospels because they find that the Gospels don't always agree on details. But if you and I went to the same football game and told about it afterwards, our stories would certainly differ. Which story would be right? They both would be because each describes how we saw the game from our different perspectives.

The four Gospels were written by four different people about the life of one person: Jesus.

Mark was probably the first Gospel written and seems to be written to or for Gentiles (non-Jews) to show that Jesus was the Son of God. Mark's writings were used by both Matthew and Luke in their Gospels.

Luke was probably the second Gospel written and seems to have been written for the Greeks to show that Jesus was a universal savior.

Matthew was probably written third and seems to have been written to prove to the Jews that Jesus fulfilled the prophecies of the coming Jewish Messiah.

John was written last as an instruction book for the early Church and may have been written to be memorized.

The four Gospels are the story of Jesus' birth, teaching, death and resurrection. What wonderful stories they are!

10th Sunday After Pentecost

"THE ECHO"

There was a story told many years ago about a boy who was always saying nasty things to other people. His mother took him to the mountains on vacation one summer. They went walking in a valley and stopped along the way for a rest.

The mother said, "Son, very often what you say will come back to you. Here is a good place to understand that lesson. You call here and a sound will come back to you."

It sounded interesting, so the boy shouted, "Hello!" Sure enough, back came, "Hello!" The boy was excited. He called, "Where are you?" Back came, "Where are you?" This made the boy angry because he thought someone was playing a joke on him. He called out. "Tell me who you are or I'll fight you!" The words came back in the same insulting tone.

The mother finally said, "Son, please tell him you like him and see what he says." The son shouted, "I like you." Sure enough, back came the words, "I like you." The boy was now very happy.

Of course this is only a story and the words coming back were really an echo. Have any of you ever experienced an echo?

One thing is surely true. If we meet people with courtesy, we get back the same. Kindness begets kindness and love begets love. That is a wonderful truth in this world that the echo reminds us to think about.

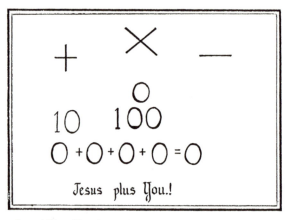

Jesus plus You.!

11th Sunday After Pentecost

"ADDITION"

What is one plus one? Answer: 2. What is two plus two? Answer: 4. Good. Now for a much more difficult addition problem. Add together 62,000 flowers, 2 million trips covering 5 million miles and one hive and what do you get.? Answer: one pound of honey.

Yes, it takes all that addition to make one pound of honey. Bee experts tell us that the sweetness of 62,000 clover blooms is required to produce just one pound of pure clover honey. To gather that much, the bees make a total of nearly 2 million trips flying about 5 million miles. That seems like a lot of work for one pound of honey.

It is true not only of honey, but of most good things in life. They don't just happen, they must be worked on to happen. Bees show us that by doing a little at a time, we can eventually get the job done.

"Righteousness" means being fair or just or true. But being righteous doesn't just happen; it takes effort. Nothing is necessarily born fair or just or true. If people want to become righteous, they need to put their minds and hearts to it.

We need to work at being fair, just and true. The bees teach us that when we make a start, even if we can do only a little at a time, we are headed in the right direction and will reach our goal.

44

12th Sunday After Pentecost

"VIP"

What does "VIP" mean? Answer: "very important person."

Children are very important people to Jesus. Once his disciples wanted Jesus to send the children home so that the adults could get closer to hear him. Jesus would have none of that. He said, "Let the children come to me."

There is another story of the young boy who helped Jesus when a crowd of nearly 5000 people became hungry while listening to Jesus talk. The boy gave his lunch of two fish and five slices of bread to Jesus. Jesus blessed the small lunch and shared it and the whole crowd was able to have enough to eat! That miracle happened because a little boy was willing to share. He was the VIP that day.

You, each one of you, is a VIP in the eyes of Jesus and the mind of God. The wonderful thing is that Jesus loves each one of you personally. That is why baptism and dedication of children are such important symbols and acts in the church. Baptism or dedication is a symbol of God's gracious love reaching out to the child. It isn't magic. God does not reject children who haven't been baptized either. We need the symbol of water for ourselves, not for God. The water reminds us that we are VIPs and that each of us must make his or her own decision about God, when we grow old enough to do so.

13th Sunday After Pentecost

"WHAT IS WORSHIP?"

Every Sunday morning, in churches large and small, in open country and in villages and cities, people come together for what we call "worship." Worship has to do with God. Worship is devotion, or telling God that God is more important to us than anything else is. In simple terms, in worship God meets us and we meet God on a spiritual level, and we express how important God is to us.

At home we often pray to God, but there we generally do not worship. Prayer is the conversation of the person's heart with God. Prayer is not the same as worship, although prayer can be a part of worship. In worship we concentrate on God, not on ourselves.

We don't go to church to "get something out of it." The reason for going to church is to give praise to God and to thank God. In worship we turn our minds and hearts to God. We have an order of worship which helps us turn our hearts to God. We don't just come into church Sunday morning and say, "I'm going to worship," and then only sit there and do nothing.

Each Sunday is a miracle, when people all over the world gather to praise God. They may come tired, confused, sad, afraid, doubting. They lay their lives before God and listen; then they depart for home changed persons.

We all need this miracle every week because our memories are short and our faith is weak. Praise God for the weekly miracle of worship.

14th Sunday After Pentecost

"CANDLES"

In John 8:12, Jesus says, "I am the light of the world." The candles we use in church are a symbol of the eternal presence of God and a reminder that Jesus is the light of the world for us.

Lamps have been used in worship for thousands of years. At one time they were only round bowls with a wick and some material that would burn. In the temple at Jerusalem the lamps were made from gold and were very elaborate.

With the development of wax, candles became more convenient to use in church. Today we use candles in church instead of burning lamps.

There are generally two candles used during the worship service. These two candles represent the two-fold nature of Jesus. Jesus was both human and divine.

Some churches use 14 candles because fourteen is a multiple of seven, and seven is an especially sacred number. There are seven days in a week; Sunday comes every seventh day. Another reason seven is special is because it is the sum of three, which symbolizes the trinity, and four, the four quarters of the earth.

However many candles we use in church during our worship service, they are there to remind us that Jesus is the light of the world and that God is always with us.

15th Sunday After Pentecost

"THE SHIP"

One symbol of the church is a ship. The word "nave" comes from the Latin word for ship. In the large cathedrals of Europe and many large churches in our own country, the nave is the long central hall, and the narthex is a room or vestibule leading to the nave of the building.

The symbol of the church as a ship comes from the idea that the church helps us sail unharmed through all the difficulties of life; life is sometimes compared to the sea. One of the disciples of Jesus, Jude, is said by tradition to have traveled far with Simon on missionary journeys. Therefore the symbol for Jude is also a ship.

Whatever the symbols or names for the different parts of a church building, you and I know that the church is a place where people come together to worship. In a real sense, the church is a spiritual hospital ship where we can go to heal our souls and to learn to face and enjoy life.

Through its various ministries, the church supports us through life so we can face difficulties with courage and share in faith our joys with others.

16th Sunday After Pentecost

"THE ALTAR"

The use of the altar as a center of worship goes back at least 2000 years before Jesus' birth, when it was a simple stone. No Christian altar in the material sense was mentioned in the New Testament.

In early Christian churches what we call the altar was really a table. Today many churches are going back to the use of tables instead of altars. The first Christians met together to eat, and offerings of food and money were placed on the table. The cross above the table was a reminder of the sacrifice Jesus had made for them and for you and me. His sacrifice brings us into a loving relationship with God.

Later the early Christians began to store relics under the table when they no longer ate together. Relics are human bones or objects kept as a memorial of a saint or martyr. In time so many relics were placed under the table that some were sticking out; so they enclosed the table. (You wouldn't want your minister to fall over bones that were sticking out from under the table, would you?) After a while some people considered these tables to be altars and that is why we have altars in many churches today.

Catholic churches still keep relics in the altar and believe that Communion is a sacrifice — hence the need for an altar.

Whether we use an altar or a table as the center of worship in church, we are reminded of how important Jesus is to each one of us.

17th Sunday After Pentecost

"SONGS AND THE CHOIR"

In most churches we sing hymns during the worship service. Music is used in church for the purpose of honoring God. It is an aid to worship.

Hymns unite people into a common fellowship because we are doing something together when we sing. Hymns bring forth feelings fitting for worship and the love of God.

The processional or first hymn in the worship service is especially for the adoration of God. Singing the first hymn is something that the congregation does together in preparation for worship.

In many churches the Gloria Patri is sung as the people of God give praise.

In churches that have a choir, the choir often sings an anthem during the service. The choir furnishes another form of expressing praise.

Often churches sing a hymn after the offering is received, a hymn that is familiar to the congregation. This hymn helps us dedicate our whole lives to the glory and service of God.

A recessional or last hymn generally followed by a prayer of benediction is used to end the service. This last hymn gives the people a way to say "yes" to any decisions of faith they feel. It is a form of dedication of one's self to God and saying, "Yes, God, I really adore and worship you and want my life to reflect that commitment."

AMEN

18th Sunday After Pentecost

"AMEN"

Romans 15:33 reads, "The God of Peace be with you. Amen."

There are actually four uses for the word "amen" in the Bible. Amen is a "transliteration" from both the Hebrew and the Greek. A transliteration is taking the sound and meaning of a word from one language and using it as part of another language. "OK" is an example; many languages now use "OK" as part of their everyday speech.

Here are the four uses of the word amen in the Bible:

1. Amen is used to agree with what is said. People in the Bible used amen to adopt as their own what had been said. We find this usage in the Psalms. We sometimes use it that way today: "Amen — I agree with you."

2. Amen sometimes is used to give strength to one's own prayers. Paul used the word this way a great deal. It was like saying, "So be it."

3. Amen is also used sometimes as an introduction. In this sense it means "truly," as in, "Truly I say unto you."

4. Amen is used at the close of a statement to mean "the end" or "I mean this." It is used at the end of songs or hymns this way.

We can begin to understand, then, that amen has different uses both in the Bible and for us today. It is a nice word to have and to use. Understanding the different uses of amen makes it even more useful to us. AMEN.

"PRAYER"

Some people have been heard to say, "The only thing I can do about this situation is to pray about it." Prayer may well be the only thing we can do in some situations, but prayer is also the greatest thing we can do! Prayer helps us to step back and allows God to step into our lives and give direction. To pray is to open all the possibilities before us and to say, "God, which is in my best interest?"

Prayer reminds us that God is always with us.

Prayer reminds us that God works through us.

Prayer reminds us that God can be in charge, if we allow.

Prayer calms our spirits and soothes our emotions.

Prayer does work.

Prayer is one of the greatest actions we can take.

When Jesus told us to "pray without ceasing" what he was asking was not that we spend all our time on our knees, but rather that we live our lives in a prayerful attitude all the time. A prayerful attitude is one in which we behave as though God is really in charge of our lives.

We can "pray without ceasing" by living lives in which God works through us to let the world know of God's love.

To be loving is to be in prayer.

To get on our knees regularly helps us remember where that love originates.

"THE BIBLE IN ENGLISH"

We take it for granted that we are able to read the Bible in English. But that hasn't always been so. Before 1525 A.D. you couldn't find a Bible in English, and before 1440 A.D. you couldn't even find a printed Bible in any language.

In 1440 the printing press was invented in Europe. Before that time, all Bibles were hand written and therefore very few people owned a Bible. Monks in monasteries hand-copied Bibles, and it was a long, tedious job to complete one copy.

Finally in 1525 the first English translation of the New Testament was done. But a lot of church people were very unhappy that some other people were translating the Bible. In fact, an Oxford scholar by the name of Wycliffe translated some of the Bible into English in 1382, and he was condemned by church officials for doing it.

King James of England ordered an English translation of the Bible in 1611. Fifty scholars working together produced the King James Version of the Bible. The language of the King James Version was so beautiful that it influenced the English language.

There are many modern versions of the Bible today. Many of these versions are attempts to make the Bible easier to read and understand.

That is the key word: read. The Bible doesn't do us any good unless we read it. Find a Bible version you like, open it and read. God's word will open up for you.

"TROUBLE WITH THE OLD TESTAMENT?"

Many people have trouble understanding some of the stories of the Old Testament. The reason is that they get caught up in details first and forget the big picture.

The Old Testament is a love story. God is the same God of love in both the Old Testament and the New Testament. When we read the stories about God getting angry or killing people, what we are reading are stories about people who were wishing such and who put their wishes into the mouth of God.

Don't we do the same kind of thing all the time? We want something, so we quote someone whom we think is important to prove our point. We often have an opinion but are afraid nobody will listen to us, so we find others who have the same opinion and quote them.

The God of the Old Testament is seen through the eyes of people who had not experienced God's love in Jesus. They saw judgement and that was their limitation. It often becomes our limitation as well.

The Bible was written by people who were inspired by the Holy Spirit, but it was also written through the hands of people who had the same limitations you and I have.

Praise God for loving us without any qualifications or limitations we might bring up.

"SOLOMON'S TEMPLE"

In the Book of I Kings in the Old Testament, we learn about David's son Solomon who followed David as king of Israel. Solomon was king from 969-922 B.C.

Solomon one day looked down from his beautiful palace and saw the tent tabernacle where people went to worship God. He decided to build a house for the Lord.

Why do you think people were worshipping in a tent? Answer: Because while they lived in the wilderness for 40 years they moved frequently and lived in tents and their church was also a movable tent.

It took seven years to build the house for the Lord, or the temple. With walls 10 feet thick, it stood for 400 years. It was a beautiful building and later came to be the center of worship for the Israelites.

Today people frequently call churches "Houses of the Lord." One mistake people sometimes make, however, is to think they can worship only in church buildings. We need to remember that God lives not only in churches but everywhere. We cannot confine God to a building.

God especially lives in our hearts. The New Testament tells us that each one of us is a "temple of God." How can that be? When we are loving and caring, the presence of God is there because loving and caring come from God.

Each of us can decide to treat our bodies and live our lives in such a way as to be worthy temples of God.

"PERFECT ATTENDANCE"

It is fun sometimes to play with statistics. They can be used to show awesome accomplishments without our feeling we need to do the same. Some examples:

Roland E. Doab, a member of St. Paul's United Church of Christ in Columbia, Illinois, on March 23, 1980, completed 3200 consecutive Sundays of worship without missing a single Sunday. That unbroken period of time is more than 61 years!

The greatest number of Christmas cards sent out by one person is 62,824. They were sent by Werner Erhard of San Francisco, California, in December 1975.

The tallest Christmas tree was a 221 foot Douglas Fir erected in Seattle, Washington, in December 1950.

You and I are not asked to attend church the most Sundays in a row, as worthy as that is. We are not asked to send out the most Christmas cards, as interesting as that may be. We are not asked to have the tallest Christmas tree.

God asks of you and me to be who we are — you to be you and me to be me. We are measured by how close we come to being the loving, caring and forgiving persons God created us to be. We are created as individuals whom God loves individually. What a wonderful God we worship.

"OLD FAITHFUL"

The favorite geyser in Yellowstone National Park is "Old Faithful." Every 64.5 minutes, with a loud roar Old Faithful shoots up a tall column of steam and water into the air 150 feet. Every time the geyser spouts it uses 10 to 12 gallons of water in a wonderful display. There are geysers that spout higher, but Old Faithful seems to be everyone's favorite.

Can you guess why? Answer: Because it is faithful. You don't have to wait for long periods of time wondering when it will spout off. It is wonderful to be faithful.

God wants each one of us to be faithful. How can you be faithful to God?

— by praying regularly

— by loving others and yourself

— by being kind and forgiving.

Old Faithful can be a useful symbol and example for us. Being faithful is a wonderful quality to have.

Who is the most faithful? God, of course! God will never leave or forsake us. We can depend on God. The Bible is a record of God's faithfulness in spite of the many times we people became unfaithful or fell away. When God seems far away, we can be sure who moved. It was us, not God. God is always faithful!

"TRYING TO HELP"

Sometimes when we want to help others they don't want our help or the situation backfires. We need to continue our desire to help and yet realize that we will not always do the "right" or correct thing. Being perfect, correctly translated, doesn't mean doing no wrong; it literally means "doing the best" we can.

There is a story out of India about elephants and people which illustrates this idea. Elephants in one of the tribal villages were chasing people off their threshing floors and eating the rice they left behind. What to do?

The missionary living nearby purchased fire crackers and borrowed a bow and some arrows. He tied a fire cracker on each of several arrows, lighted the fire crackers one by one and shot them in the direction of the elephant herd. The elephants ran in one direction and he in another. The village was now safe from the elephants because they had moved far away. Unfortunately, the elephants simply moved to another village to find rice to eat. One village was helped but another village was hurt.

The missionary did the best he could, and his best did not help everyone. Life is very often like that. However, Jesus tells us to be perfect, that is, to try our very best. That is all which is asked of us. We cannot be perfect in the sense of never doing harm to anyone or ourselves, but we can be perfect in using love as the force to help us always do our very best.

26th Sunday After Pentecost

"LIFE AS A MIRACLE"

Life is nothing short of a miracle. Just look at what our body does for us. In 24 hours, your heart beats 103,689 times; your blood travels 168,000 miles; you breathe 23,040 times; you inhale 438 cubic feet of air; you eat 3 pounds of food; you drink 2.9 quarts of liquids; and you speak 4000 words, including a lot of unnecessary ones.

Jesus said in John 15, "I am the true vine and you are the branches." What a wonderful thought! The difference between vines and people is that while the branch has no choice about being part of the vine, we as people with our remarkable bodies have a choice about being with Jesus.

Our body is important to us and it is a miracle. But our souls are also just as much a part of us, and no less a miracle. When Jesus talked about the vine and the branches, he was talking in a spiritual sense. Our souls are the part of us which we do not see but which we feel and experience.

We care for our bodies by eating, drinking and sleeping. We care for our souls by prayer, Bible study, attending Sunday school and church and by loving God, others and ourselves.

Life is a miracle. Let us show our thankfulness for that miracle by taking care of our bodies and our souls.

27th Sunday After Pentecost

"THE MEANING OF FAITH"

Job is one of the most celebrated writings in the Bible, but perhaps is the least known or understood. The story of Job is about a period of history about 700 B.C. but it wasn't written until around 580-540 B.C.

Many people feel Job was written to deal with the question of why good or righteous people suffer. But the main question of Job seems to be, "What is the meaning of faith?"

In the story Job has a lot of troubles. He has so many serious troubles that one easily begins to feel sorry for him. He shouts out, "I'm not to blame!" How many times have we tried that one ourselves! When things don't go our way, we certainly like to complain, don't we?

The main theme of Job is that God is completely in charge of the world and that we are all accountable to God. God's grace gave Job life and restored his life. Job is told, "Take a look at yourself. What can you do on your own?" And of course he could do nothing on his own. Job asks the question, "What is faith?" and he receives a strange kind of answer. The answer is that God is the source of all. That is not the answer Job wanted and it may not be the answer we want, but it is the answer we get.

The Book of Job was written to look at the human situation at its worst. Job was led to God and the need for grace. He couldn't do anything on his own. You and I experience that same grace in Jesus. Faith is not the work of us, but rather a gift of God. Faith is the belief that God is in charge and knows what God is doing.

PART II

CHURCH DAYS

"CHRISTMAS"

In 1818 a priest named Father Joseph Mohr wrote three six-line stanzas the afternoon before Christmas. He then asked his friend Franz Gruber, who was the organist at St. Nicholas Church in Salzburg, to set the words to music. There was, however, a big problem. The organ was not working. The river nearby had flooded the church and the water had damaged the organ.

Later that evening, for Christmas Eve Midnight Mass, Father Mohr sang the melody of the music his friend had composed and played his old guitar. Gruber sang with the choir.

That is how "Silent Night" was sung for the first time that evening.

Father Mohr got into trouble with the church officials for playing his guitar in church. In fact, he was transferred twelve times in eight years and finally ended up serving a very small church that could hardly support him. When he died, he was buried in a grave for paupers or poor people.

But his carol "Silent Night" lives on to comfort and give peace to millions during the Christmas season. We thank Father Mohr for his faith and the gift of "Silent Night" that he gave to the world and to you and to me.

"SANTA CLAUS"

In the 4th century, 1500 years ago, there was a bishop of Myra (in Asia Minor) who is reported to have done very helpful things for sailors and school children. His name was Saint Nicholas. We can read stories about the many wonderful deeds he did. Around Christmas time it is said that he was especially nice in giving very poor children presents of clothing to keep them warm during the cold winter.

Because of St. Nicholas, the name "Nicholas" later was often given to persons and places in many countries. Several last names come from Nicholas: Nichols, Nicholson, Colson and Collins are a few.

The Dutch who settled in New York called St. Nicholas "Sinter Klaas" in their language. The English pronounced "Sinter Klaas" as "Santa Claus." He was said to love to leave goodies in children's shoes.

Saint Nick's clothes gradually changed from a long robe to a red and white outfit, but he kept his pipe and fur trim. In 1822 Clement Moore wrote the poem "The Night Before Christmas" and made St. Nick jolly, plump and with a white beard.

So today our Santa Claus is based on a real person, a saint who went about doing good.

New Year's Day

"THE NEW YEAR"

We can look at the New Year as a new book. Day by day and page by page we write our own book. What kind of book are you going to write this year?

Will it be a better book than last year? Of course we all hope so. Saying things are going to be different is to make New Year's resolutions. But New Year's resolutions are good only if we carry them out.

There is a story about a little girl who was drawing pictures with a pen and ink. She drew a picture of a cat without a tail. One of her friends asked, "Where is the tail?" The little girl replied, "Oh, the tail is still in the ink bottle."

At the end of this year we don't want our resolutions to still be waiting, so we need to begin today to carry them out.

God wants us to live loving, joyful and peaceful lives. But it is really up to each one of us. What kind of book do you want to write about yourself this New Year?

"ASH WEDNESDAY"

We have been celebrating the Epiphany season since January 6. The color we used as the symbol for that season is white. Remember, we said that Epiphany means to reveal who Jesus was.

Today is Ash Wednesday, the beginning of Lent. The color we use during Lent is purple or violet, colors that symbolize humility, sorrow and royalty. From Ash Wednesday to Easter there are 40 days, not counting Sundays.

Ash Wednesday got its name during the Middle Ages. The minister would keep the palm leaves used on Palm Sunday and burn them. The next year, on the first day of Lent he would rub the ashes from the burnt palms on the foreheads of people worshipping. Hence Ash Wednesday.

The date of Easter varies from year to year and is called a variable feast day, so Ash Wednesday varies also. Easter falls on the first Sunday after the first full moon after the first day of spring. It can vary from March 23 to April 25 in different years.

Ashes are symbols which remind us:

— that God creates from the dust of the ground.

— that we are to be aware of the hurts of others, and

— that from ashes God brings goodness.

Ash Wednesday is a time of preparing our hearts and minds for the Lenten season. Happy Ash Wednesday!

"MAUNDY THURSDAY"

Maundy Thursday comes from the word which means washing the feet of Jesus' disciples on the Thursday before Easter. Jesus washed his disciples' feet to show that he wanted to serve them. He served them with all that he had, including his very life.

Some of the disciples didn't want him to wash their feet, but when he told them that he had to or they could not follow him, they all agreed. In an upper room after they had all eaten, Jesus washed and dried the feet of each disciple.

Today some churches still practice the foot washing ceremony, especially on Maundy Thursday.

Also, in some parts of the world foot washing is still practiced. One missionary visited a rural village by walking many miles over a dusty road. When he got to the village where he would preach, the leader of that village brought water and washed his feet. Oh, did that feel good!

You and I can remember Maundy Thursday by doing nice things for other people to show them that God loves them and we love them. Jesus' washing his disciples' feet shows that we all can help others. Nobody is too good to help others. We thank Jesus for that lesson.

"THANKSGIVING"

Thanksgiving Day is a very American holiday. The Pilgrims came to America in 1620. It was a strange land and they had much to learn about it. During the first year one half of them had died. Now they were facing a very cold winter, but they had managed to grow a small harvest and they wanted to thank God for this harvest.

The Pilgrims invited their Indian friend, Chief Massasoit, to eat with them. The Chief brought ninety hungry warriors along. As a result the five women of Plymouth had to feed 145 people.

The people dined well. They ate venison, wild fowl, eel, shellfish, lobster, corn and dried fruits. Their Indian friends also brought food, including turkey, as their share of the feast. We associate turkey with Thanksgiving today.

What a feast it was! It went on for three days. There were many prayers of thanks, sermons and songs. There were no utensils to eat with except knives for cutting food. They ate with their fingers or scraped up food with clamshell spoons.

On that first Thanksgiving in 1621 the people were thankful for all they had. As we celebrate Thanksgiving this year, let us also be thankful for what we have. The secret to happiness and joy is in expressing what we are and who we are and in being thankful for what we have. When we recognize God as the source of all good things and all love, then we know whom to thank.

PART III
OTHER SPECIAL DAYS

1st Day Of April

"APRIL FOOL'S DAY"

April Fool's Day is an interesting date to learn about. Ancient Rome observed a similar day on March 25.

April Fool's Day is related to the vernal equinox at the beginning of spring. About that time a sudden change in the weather can make us think spring climate is here, but generally there is more bad weather to come. In other words, we are fooled into thinking spring has come.

The equinox occurs when the sun crosses the equator, making day and night equal in length. The vernal equinox occurs about March 21 and the autumnal equinox about September 22 or 23.

The word "april" comes from ancient Rome and means "open." The first flowers bloom in Rome about the first of April.

Some people play jokes on others on April Fool's Day. In France the person fooled is called a "fish." In Scotland the victim is called a "cuckoo."

April and spring are times for us to concentrate on being open persons. We can learn to be open to God and to others. We can learn to open our hearts, minds and souls to God's love for us and let God's love flow through us.

Boy Scout Sunday

"THE BOY SCOUTS"

On Boy Scout Sunday we recognize the Boy Scouts of America and the Boy Scouts around the world. There are more than 15 million Boy Scouts throughout 120 countries of the world.

Lord Baden-Powell started the Boy Scouts in Great Britain in 1907. Boy Scouts were brought to the U.S.A. in 1909 after a scout in Great Britain did a good deed for William Boyce, an American businessman lost in a London fog. As a result, Mr. Boyce introduced Boy Scouting to our country.

The Boy Scouts of America were incorporated on February 8, 1910, which is the date now observed throughout the country as Boy Scout Anniversary Day. The President of the United States is Honorary President of the BSA and former presidents are Honorary Vice-Presidents.

The Boy Scouts throughout the years have proved themselves useful citizens, giving service in times of flood, fire, hurricane and other disasters as well as helping at parades and civic gatherings.

The twelfth part of the Scout Law is, "A scout is reverent." A boy scout is reverent toward God. He is faithful in his religious duties and respects the beliefs of others in matters of customs and religion. All people are created by the same God, and boy scouts believe all people are equal before God.

Children's Day

"CHILDREN'S DAY"

Many Protestant churches in the United States celebrate Children's Day on the second Sunday in June. On that day children are sometimes promoted from one Sunday School class to the next class.

Here are two poems about children, one for sons and one for daughters:

SONS

When God wanted to create
Joy and sorrow in one package,
The bringer of sadness and pride,
When God wanted to create
Things that like to play baseball
And climb high trees,
When God wanted to create,
A small hand reaching out
And gripping your big hand,
When God wanted to create
Someone who would come up and say
"Can I borrow the car tonight?"
When God wanted to create
Someone who wants to cry when hurt,
But doesn't want to show pain,
When God wanted to create
Someone who would come up
And whisper in your ear
"I love you Mom/Dad"
God created SONS.

DAUGHTERS

When God wanted to create
Bundles of energy and enthusiasm
That would bring happiness,
When God wanted to create
A thing Dads would be proud of
And Moms would beam about,
When God wanted to create
Things that would tease strong boys
And run away from small worms,
When God wanted to create
Things to wear beautiful clothes
And keep parents up at night waiting
When God wanted to create
Joy and sorrow in one package,
A beautiful package that none
Would trade for anything else
In the world,
God created DAUGHTERS.

Communion Sunday

"COMMUNION AND BAPTISM"

The word "Sacrament" means "something sacred." In Protestant churches we celebrate two Sacraments: The Lord's Supper, also called Holy Communion, and Baptism. Both of these sacraments go back to the life of Jesus. Jesus was baptized by his cousin John and that act marked the beginning of Jesus' ministry.

Both the Lord's Supper and Baptism are symbolic acts. That is, they stand for something spiritual, something we do not see but can feel and experience.

In Baptism we use water. What we do not see are the hopes and dreams and the plans of the parents. We do not see the Church of which the child will become a member, for the Church Universal goes around the world and includes the past and the future. We do not see God's gracious love reaching out and touching the child. In Baptism we sprinkle with water three times, in the name of the Father, Son and Holy Spirit (see Matthew 28:19).

In the Lord's Supper we use bread and wine. The bread is the symbol for the body of Jesus and the wine is the symbol for the sacrifice Jesus made for us with his death. The Lord's Supper is a memorial feast during which we remember Jesus' last meal with his disciples. As we take Communion we also become part of that meal.

The symbols of the Sacraments give meaning to water and food every day in our lives. We give thanks for the Sacraments.

Confirmation Sunday

"JOINING THE CHURCH"

We want to talk to the confirmands today. What are you joining today? You are joining the Church. The Church is an organized effort to demonstrate God's loving concern for the world. The Church is not perfect, but it is the best we have.

What does the Church ask from you?

1. The Church wants your support. Some people think that the church only asks for money. That is not true. The Church asks for your sense of dedication and a gift of your time and talent.

2. The church wants you to pray.

3. The church wants you to be faithful to Jesus.

What do you receive from the Church?

1. Service and help throughout the trials and joys of your life.

2. Christian fellowship.

3. Opportunities to demonstrate what God means to you.

Congratulations to you on completing your confirmation instructions, and welcome to the Christian Church and to this church. The Church will be as loving as you are because you are now part of the Church.

Father's Day

"FATHER'S DAY"

Father's Day came from an idea that Mrs. John Brice Dodd had in 1910. She talked to her minister in Spokane, Washington, about some way to honor fathers. A few churches began the celebration and the idea spread.

In 1924 President Coolidge asked people to celebrate Father's Day in honor of their fathers. Ever since, Father's Day has been celebrated on the third Sunday in June.

Here is a poem to Fathers:

FATHERS

When God wanted to create
A person who could tuck children in bed
And tell them scary stories,
When God wanted to create
A person to get excited when his son
Ran a touchdown,
When God wanted to create
A person bursting with pride
When his duaghter had the lead in the school play,
When God wanted to create
A person little children could look up to,
And tall boys could look across at,
When God wanted to create
A big hand for a sad child
To reach out and take and hold,
When God wanted to create
A support for mothers and an
Answer to the question, "Go ask your . . ."
When God wanted to create strength
And weakness, love and discipline,
God created FATHERS.

The Fourth Of July

"INDEPENDENCE DAY"

The Fourth of July celebrates the formal adoption of the Declaration of Independence. The Declaration of Independence was drafted or written on July 2, 1776, and formally adopted July 4, 1776. In it a group of Americans declared that we were independent from England.

What were we free from? What are we free to do? We are free from the rule or domination of foreign powers. But freedom also carries with it responsibilities.

The motto of the United States of America is "In God We Trust." This motto was adopted by the early leaders of our country in the days when we were a weak and struggling nation. The founding leaders felt it absolutely necessary to trust in a greater power than themselves for the making and preserving of the nation.

Unfortunately, with an increase in wealth, power and prestige in this country there has been a decrease in the feeling that we need to depend on God. God is often left out of the decision-making process.

On Independence Day it is helpful to remember our motto, "In God We Trust." God is to come even before our country. Nations come and nations go, but God is always with us. We can be both loyal citizens and proud of our country and also citizens of God's kingdom at the same time.

Girl Scout Sunday

"THE GIRL SCOUTS"

Today is Girl Scout Sunday. The Girl Scouts were started in the United States by Juliette Gordon Low. Her nickname was "Daisy." Daisy was born in 1860, just before the Civil War broke out, and grew up in Savannah, Georgia.

In 1886 Daisy married William Low. During her wedding a guest threw rice at her and some went into her ear. When a doctor tried to remove the rice, she became deaf in that ear. The sad thing was that she could only partially hear out of the other ear. But that did not stop Daisy!

She traveled a lot and while in England she met the founder of the Boy Scouts. His sister had organized the Girl Scouts in England. Daisy brought the idea back to the U.S.A.

On March 12, 1912, 18 girls met at Daisy's house to form a Girl Scout troop. They made their own uniforms. From that small beginning Girl Scouts have grown to the point that we now have girl scouts in all the states and all the larger cities of the country.

March 12 is set aside as the birthday of Girl Scouting in the U.S.A. Daisy is remembered as a woman who worked for peace and good will among all people.

We thank her for bringing the idea of Girl Scouts to the United States and for starting the first Girl Scout troop in this country.

76

Labor Sunday

"LABOR DAY"

The first Monday in September we celebrate as Labor Day. It is a day chosen by a few countries in the world to honor work and those involved especially in jobs of physical labor.

Colorado passed the first Labor Day Act in 1887. Other states soon did the same. Finally in 1894, Congress passed a bill making Labor Day a legal holiday throughout the nation. Now Labor Day is celebrated in the United States and in Canada on the first Monday in September. In some other countries May first is the special day honoring the laboring class.

Labor Day is an important day in the U.S.A. because around this time we start back to school, churches and other organizations begin their fall schedules, and summer begins to feel as if it is over.

It is important to honor labor. In some nations physical labor is looked down upon. Parents try to get their children educated so they don't have to "get their hands dirty." How sad! Without working people we would not have any food to eat, cars to drive or even toys to play with.

In God's plan all honest work is honored. Today we particularly thank God for all the people who work hard to help make the things that make life safe, pleasant and comfortable.

Memorial Day Sunday

"MEMORIAL DAY"

Memorial Day began as a remembrance of soldiers and sailors of the Civil War. In 1866 women in the South placed flowers on the graves of the dead. In 1868 a Union Veterans' organization set aside May 30 to remember the dead Union soldiers. The day was known as "Decoration Day" because the graves were decorated with flowers. You may still hear some people refer to Memorial Day as Decoration Day. Many Southern states celebrate their own Memorial Day as well as the national day.

Today on Memorial Day Sunday we pay respects to all of those who died in all the wars since the Civil War.

In 1971 Memorial Day was set as the last Monday of May so we will always celebrate it on that date. It is a time to remember those who died in the war so that you and I might live in a free country.

We not only remember, but we give thanks for those lives sacrificed for freedom. We are not free "just because." We are free because people have been willing to defend our country against others who wanted us under their control. Some of our people paid the full price, their very lives. We give them thanks and remember them on this special day on which we decorate their graves.

May God bless their gift of life and the service they gave to our country.

Memorial Sunday

"MEMORIAL SUNDAY"

In the Jewish tradition, mourning is essentially a process of learning not to expect the presence of a person who has died. There is one month of deep grief followed by eleven months of remembrance and healing. This tradition recognizes the fact that the emotional acceptance of the death of someone dear takes time and work and pain. We cannot just wish pain away.

Today we remember those loved ones who died last year. Some will be more special to us than others, but to God they are all special.

It is hard to die, and it will always be so, even when we have accepted death as an integral part of life, because dying means giving up life on this earth and the things we did with our loved ones who died. Death is the ultimate of separations, and unlike others, we have little choice as to whether or when it will occur.

The Apostle Paul tells us to hold on to our faith despite the mysteries of life. We know that there is not total death. Only the body dies. The spirit is eternal. Death is another beginning, a new birth into a new state of existence. When the body ceases to be, the spirit emerges free and unencumbered.

We think about each of those who have died this past year, and we remember the words of Paul, "For if I live or die, I am the Lord's." If we are surrounded with love, death makes no difference because in both heaven and here on earth our goal is the same: to love and be loved.

We remember and thank God for the lives of those who died this past year.

Mother's Day

"MOTHER'S DAY"

Today is Mother's Day. It is appropriate to give special thought to mothers on their day. Since Mother's Day was recognized by the U.S. Congress in 1914, we have set aside this day to give thanks to all mothers.

The following is a story, a sad story. Life itself is often sad. The purpose of the story is to hold high the ideal of motherhood and the responsibility of children to remember their mothers.

Not too many years ago a rural family lived in one of our Western states. The parents struggled hard to give their children advantages they had not had. Unfortunately the father was killed in an accident early in the life of the family. The mother continued to operate the small ranch and rear the three boys and girl. She worked hard and all the children continued their education beyond high school, married and moved to distant parts of the country. None thought it necessary to stay in contact with their mother or each other.

At the small ranch their mother grew older and more lonely. She wanted desperately to receive a letter from at least one of her children. She was on a rural route but maintained a post office box in town, driving to town each day to open the box hopefully. Each day the key turned in the lock, only to add to her growing disappointment. For 15 years she opened box number 112 and for 15 years she did not find a single letter from her children.

One day very unexpectedly, her daughter and one of the brothers met in a distant town. News was exchanged. The two realized that none of them had been in contact with their mother in recent years. Yet they readily admitted she was the force behind their social and economic success in life. They decided to write their mother and send her a gift.

The two contacted their brothers, who agreed to join in. None of them were angry with their mother; they had just gotten involved with their own families and did not think of mother so far away and out in the country. So they glued photos of the four children, their families and homes into a photo album and sent it on to their mother.

The day the album arrived, the postmaster was excited. He waited all day for his friend to come because he guessed the package was probably from one of her children. He knew well of her hopes because he had tried to convince her many times that the postal box and her daily trips to town were not necessary. He had promised that when letters arrived, they would be promptly delivered. But she wanted a letter as soon as it arrived and she waited daily while the mail was sorted into the boxes. He often saw her sad face as she waited.

Throughout the day the postmaster glanced out the window, but the mother did not come. When closing time arrived, he decided to drive out to the ranch and take his friend the package from her children. He didn't know how important it was, but something in him told him it was very important.

Arriving at the ranch, he found all was quiet. He broke the silence by calling out, "Hello, anybody home?" No answer. On the porch he peered into the living room. On the floor lay his friend. The door was unlocked and he entered quickly to find the woman in a coma. The ambulance soon arrived and carried her off to the hospital. That evening the postmaster visited his partially-revived friend and gave her the package which he had to help her open. Large tears ran down each of her cheeks as they together turned the pages and read the notations under each photo.

The woman died quietly the next morning, knowing that her children did care. Can we say as much of our mother and ourselves?

MOTHERS

When God wanted to create
A person of beauty and
A source of strength,
When God wanted to create
A bundle of love and caring,
A package of concern and sharing,
When God wanted to create
Hands that would put bandages
On cut knees
And lips that would kiss
Away hurts;
When God wanted to create
Someone who would pray to him
And sing God's Holy Name,
God created MOTHERS.

Valentine's Day

"VALENTINE'S DAY"

Was there really a St. Valentine? On February 14, some churches celebrate the Feast of St. Valentine. In fact some historians believe there were two St. Valentines. Both were priests who were killed for what they believed. One of them lived in Rome about 300 years after the birth of Jesus. He was executed for performing Christian weddings when the Roman emperor had ordered him not to.

Valentine's Day, as a lover's festival, and the sending of valentines bears no relation to either of the St. Valentines. How, then, did St. Valentine and Valentine's Day get mixed up together?

Valentine's Day goes back before Jesus was born. In ancient Rome boys drew girls' names from a love urn on a special celebration held on February 15. The custom was introduced to England by the Romans. In order to adapt the practice to Christianity, the church changed the celebration to the day of the Feast of St. Valentine.

In 1860 in the United States, commercial greeting cards were introduced. Since then people have been sending valentine cards to one another.

You and I can use Valentine's Day to tell those we care about that we do care. All love comes from God and it is fitting that Valentine's Day be observed and used for letting others know we care.

Valentine's Day is a part of ancient history which Christians can still use to tell others of affection and love.

World Communion Sunday

"COMMUNION"

Today around the world Christians from all groups, sects and denominations celebrate the Lord's Supper as World Communion Sunday.

The bread and the wine are symbolic of Christians offering themselves, their works, their money, their material gifts and their praises to God.

The Lord's Supper, or Holy Communion, is not a sacrifice we offer in addition to the sacrifice of Jesus, but is done in remembrance of Jesus' sacrifice. It means that the Church on earth takes part in Jesus' offering in heaven. The bread is the symbol of Jesus' body and the wine is the symbol of his blood.

Communion was given to us by Jesus himself as a way to remember his death and his coming again. Communion is not a magic act. It is a miracle, a receiving of the life-giving spirit of the Risen Christ.

In the early Church the Lord's Supper was a real meal that the Christian community sat down and ate together. Eventually it became symbolic, with the use of only bread and wine instead of an entire meal.

Communion is a time in the life of the Church and in our personal lives when we receive a spiritual nourishment as we remember Jesus and his last meal with his friends. When we take part in Communion we take part in that last meal with Jesus. Today people all around the world are doing just that, taking Communion together.

Civil Air Patrol Sunday

Today is Civil Air Patrol Sunday. What is CAP? CAP is an auxiliary of the United States Air Force. CAP performs air search and rescue missions, conducts educational programs for young people and the public and encourages young men and women to take service roles in the community and to become leaders.

The CAP was organized Dec. 1, 1941 as part of the U.S. civil defense structure. The organization became a permanent peacetime institution on July 1, 1946 and a permanent civilian auxiliary of the Air Force in May 1948. CAP members are volunteers and are not paid for their services.

CAP has four missions:

1. Emergency services: the CAP flies 80% of all air searches in the USA.

2. Aerospace education to members, educators and the public.

3. Cadet program: aerospace education, moral leaderships, physical activity and drill and courtesy.

4. Senior member program: search and rescue, training of cadets, etc.

CAP has nearly 60,000 volunteer members throughout every state plus Puerto Rico and the District of Columbia.

CAP has a chaplaincy program to provide professional leadership and guidance in the religious life, morale and morals of all CAP members. CAP chaplains enhance the members' church and home training in spiritual and moral values.

Today we give thanks for the Civil Air Patrol.